MMA
MIXED MARTIAL ARTS™

BRAZILIAN JIU-JITSU

Greg Roza

WITH STEP-BY-STEP STOP-ACTION
MOVES BY *BEN DANIEL*

rosen publishing's
rosen
central®

New York

For Shihan Mike Downs, sixth-degree black belt in Isshinryu karate
—Greg Roza

Dedicated to my loving Sensei, Master Mal Perkins, 6th Dan. This wouldn't have come to fruition without the love and training you have given me over the years. Hail, Master Mal!
—Sensei Ben Daniel

Published in 2013 by The Rosen Publishing Group, Inc.
29 East 21st Street, New York, NY 10010

Copyright © 2013 by The Rosen Publishing Group, Inc.

First Edition

Descriptions of moves by Sensei Ben Daniel and Sensei Adam Mazin. "Monk Choke" move created by Adam Mazin.

This book is published only as a means of providing information on unique aspects of the history and current practice of martial arts. Neither Rosen Publishing nor the author makes any representation, warranty, or guarantee that the techniques described or photographs included in this book will be safe or effective in any self-defense situation or otherwise. You may be injured if you apply or train in the techniques of self-defense presented in this book, and neither Rosen Publishing nor the author is responsible for any such injury that may result. It is essential that you consult a parent or guardian regarding whether or not to attempt any technique described in this book. Specific self-defense techniques shown in this book may not be called for in a specific set of circumstances or under applicable federal, state, or local law. Neither Rosen Publishing nor the author makes any representation or warranty regarding the legality or appropriateness of any technique mentioned in this book.

Library of Congress Cataloging-in-Publication Data

Roza, Greg.
Brazilian jiu-jitsu/Greg Roza.
    p. cm.—(MMA: mixed martial arts)
Includes bibliographical references and index.
ISBN 978-1-4488-6965-7 (library binding)
1. Jiu-jitsu—Brazil. I. Title.
GV1114.R69 2012
796.8152—dc23

2011050290

Manufactured in the United States of America

CPSIA Compliance Information: Batch #S12YA: For further information, contact Rosen Publishing, New York, New York, at 1-800-237-9932.

CONTENTS

INTRODUCTION

Long ago, martial arts were developed by cultures across the globe for hunting, combat, and the defense of people and property. These were once everyday activities for most people. Today, martial arts training plays a large role in the preparation of law enforcement personnel and soldiers all over the world. Security guards, athletes, and even actors train in the martial arts to help them do their best in their careers.

Some people unfamiliar with the martial arts—aside from portrayals in the media—often think they are simply violent and barbaric. This couldn't be further from the

Two fighters compete at the 2010 Abu Dhabi World Jiu-Jitsu Championships.

truth. Adults, teens, and children as young as four years old train in the martial arts for numerous reasons. At the very least, it's an excellent way to stay fit. Training in a martial art teaches people how to defend themselves while building discipline and self-confidence. But that's not all. It also teaches respect and courtesy for teachers and fellow students. These traits transfer over to the everyday lives of martial art students and affect the people around them.

Some martial arts, such as kung fu, were established in ancient times. Some, such as the Korean art of tae kwon do, were developed in the past one hundred years. Others grew directly out of older forms, as is the case with the topic of this book, Brazilian jiu-jitsu.

Mixed martial arts, or MMA, is a combat sport between two athletes, most of whom have trained in two or more martial arts. Competitors are free to use any martial art technique to defeat an opponent. Many fighters hope to use kicks and punches to knock out (KO) their opponent. A referee may stop a fight if a competitor can't properly defend himself or herself; that's a technical knockout (TKO). A submission occurs when a fighter "taps out," or concedes a loss by signaling submission with a hand tap. Last, if both fighters make it through the specified number of rounds, judges decide the winner based on the points he or she earned during the fight.

A fighter who uses a single martial art may win a few fights but isn't likely to be consistently successful. There's more than one way to win a match, and a fighter who focuses on a single method is sure to lose to more knowledgeable fighters.

Some martial arts are known as "stand-up" styles. These include boxing, karate, and muay thai. Stand-up styles focus mainly on swift, powerful punches and kicks to knock out an opponent. Other weapons include elbow and knee strikes. A stand-up fighter may use more exciting attacks as well, such as jump kicks, spinning back fist punches, and flying knee kicks.

Stand-up fighters also use grappling techniques, such as a clinch, throw, or takedown. During a clinch, the two fighters hold on to each other. They do this to keep their opponent from attacking and to get the upper hand. Clinches are often used to set up a knee or elbow strike. They are also used to set up a throw or takedown. At that point, the match becomes a "ground" game.

Ground styles include wrestling and jiu-jitsu. Ground fighters often try to apply a submission hold to end a fight. This is a move that causes pain or cuts off an opponent's air supply. During a "ground and pound," a fighter gets into a position of control over an opponent and uses punches to end a fight. While stand-up and ground techniques each have their benefits, a well-rounded MMA fighter knows how to use both.

There are different theories about the origin of the Japanese martial art called jiu-jitsu. Some say it was developed by Buddhist monks in ancient India. As Buddhism spread to Southeast Asia, China, and then to Japan, so did the art of jiu-jitsu. Another theory says it originated as a form of wrestling in Mongolia and spread to China and then Japan.

Regardless of its origin, the Japanese embraced the ancient techniques. Japanese soldiers learned jiu-jitsu to prepare for unarmed combat against armed foes. By the late 1800s, jiu-jitsu transformed into a popular combat sport. Different jiu-jitsu masters developed their own styles. The combat sport judo is a martial art that focuses on the throws and takedowns of traditional jiu-jitsu.

The name "jiu-jitsu" means "the gentle art." Jiu-jitsu practitioners don't use punches and kicks to beat their opponents. Rather, they use grappling and throwing techniques. Jiu-jitsu also includes pinning techniques similar to those used in wrestling. Jiu-jitsu's effectiveness comes from the expert application of balance and leverage,

Souza was born on December 7, 1979, and grew up in Cariacica, Brazil. His early life was hard. After Souza witnessed the shooting of a good friend, his mother sent him to live with his brother in Manaus, Brazil. There, Brazilian jiu-jitsu master Henrique Machado—who trained under Carlos Gracie—saw Souza playing soccer in the street and was instantly impressed with the youth. Machado offered to train Souza. At first, Souza wasn't very interested. However, his competitiveness kicked in after getting beaten in his first class.

Soon, Machado started the Associação Sensei de Lutas Esportivas (Sensei Fighting Sports Association), or ASLE, and Souza became its best grappler. Souza improved continuously, winning several regional championships at the lower belts. His first big achievement came in 2003, when he won the brown belt division of the World Brazilian Jiu-Jitsu Championships. He won his weight division and the absolute division, submitting all but one opponent. That same year, Machado awarded Souza his black belt in Brazilian jiu-jitsu.

In 2004, Souza took second place in the black belt division of the World Championships. However, he beat Roger Gracie to become the absolute division champion. He won the fight despite suffering a serious elbow injury from an armbar by Gracie. The following year was perhaps Souza's best. He won his weight division in the ADCC, but lost to Roger Gracie in the absolute division. At the 2005 World Championships he won both his weight division and the absolute division.

In 2006, Souza moved into MMA, eager to prove his abilities outside the realm of Brazilian jiu-jitsu. He lost his first fight but then won the next ten. Souza became the 2010 Strikeforce middleweight champion by earning a unanimous decision from the judges in a win over Tim Kennedy. He defended his title against MMA great Robbie Lawler. Souza beat Lawler with a Brazilian jiu-jitsu move called a rear naked choke.

Souza also has a black belt in judo, a sport that utilizes numerous throws and takedowns. This knowledge has helped Souza, allowing him to explosively take opponents to the ground, where his Brazilian jiu-jitsu training takes over. In addition to his grappling skills, Souza has developed into an effective striker. He uses quick, accurate punches to distract his opponents before taking them to the ground. Of Souza's fourteen MMA wins, eleven of them are submissions. Several of the submissions were the result of a barrage of punches, rather than actual submission moves.

SHINYA AOKI

Known for his colorful and acrobatic style, Shinya Aoki is considered one of the best BJJ fighters in the world. He is particularly known for his "flying submissions," which are moves that require the fighter to leave his feet to put on joint locks. In fact, he has earned the nickname Tobikan Judan, which is Japanese for "the grand master of flying submissions." Aoki is very quick to administer Brazilian jiu-jitsu chokes and locks. He has a remarkable 65 percent submission record.

Aoki was born in 1983 in Shizuoka, Japan. In high school, Aoki began training in a style of judo that focuses on ground fighting and submissions, and he met with early success. He continued his judo training in college. Because of his excellent submission skills, Aoki soon became interested in Brazilian jiu-jitsu and the Russian grappling art sambo. He soon joined the Paraestra gym in Japan, which focused on MMA-style training. There, he trained under master Yuki Nakai, who had gained recognition as an accomplished MMA fighter in the Japanese Shooto organization. He's also a veteran Brazilian jiu-jitsu fighter. Aoki eventually became an assistant instructor at the Paraestra gym.

Aoki quickly became known as a fast, aggressive fighter. He has repeatedly wowed fans with flying arm locks and devastating submissions.

However, just as his fans thought he was poised to become a superstar, Aoki announced that he was leaving MMA to become a police officer. But Aoki realized he couldn't stay away from competition and quickly announced his return.

In his late twenties, Aoki has an amazing MMA record of twenty-nine wins and five losses. Of his wins, nineteen were by submission. His favorite moves are flying submissions and the "rubber guard," which requires flexibility and skill. He has been the champion of numerous Brazilian jiu-jitsu and MMA organizations, including the Shooto, Pride, and Strikeforce organizations. He is the current lightweight champion of the Japanese MMA organization Dream.

Aoki's amazing career was marred during a fight in 2009. He broke the arm of an opponent who refused to

Shinya Aoki poses proudly with his middleweight belt in March 2010.

submit to an arm lock called a hammerlock. Immediately after the fight, Aoki celebrated in an unsportsmanlike manner. As a result, he was relieved of his position as a trainer at Paraestra. However, Aoki publicly apologized for his actions. Despite this black mark on his record, the victory itself demonstrated his Brazilian jiu-jitsu dominance and dedication to success.

Despite his ups and downs, Aoki is clearly one of the best Brazilian jiu-jitsu fighters in MMA today. He is also a black belt in judo. He is currently ranked as the number four lightweight fighter in the world by several MMA associations.

B. J. PENN

B. J. Penn is one of the greatest U.S. fighters in MMA today. He is just one of two MMA fighters to win championships in two different weight classes, lightweight and heavyweight. Penn is also a Brazilian jiu-jitsu champion.

B. J. Penn was born on December 12, 1978, in Hilo, Hawaii. He began training in Brazilian jiu-jitsu when he was seventeen. One of his instructors was Ralph Gracie, grandson of Carlos Gracie. Remarkably, Penn earned his Brazilian jiu-jitsu black belt in just three years—an accomplishment that usually takes ten or more years. In 2000, Penn became the only non-Brazilian ever to win first place in the black-belt division of the World Brazilian Jiu-Jitsu Championships. After his quick rise to success in Brazilian jiu-jitsu, Penn earned the nickname the Prodigy.

Just one year later, Penn launched his MMA career. In May 2001, Penn fought Joey Gilbert in a UFC event and earned his first win by TKO. Penn wowed the MMA world by earning TKOs against his next two opponents. His next fight was against Jens Pulver for the first UFC lightweight title match. Although he made it through all five rounds, Penn lost by judges' decision.

B. J. Penn lands a blow against Diego Sanchez during UFC 107. He went on to win the match and retain his UFC lightweight championship.

Penn's first loss only inspired him to work harder. He won three of his next four UFC fights, the other ending in a draw. He briefly left the UFC to fight in a match for the Pride MMA organization. Penn's opponent was Pride lightweight champion Takanori Gomi. Early in the match, Penn demonstrated his excellent Brazilian jiu-jitsu skills. Halfway though the third round, Penn was able to force a submission using a rear naked choke—a winning move Gomi himself has been known to use. This victory was seen by many as a turning point in Penn's career.

After briefly fighting for the Pride organization, Penn returned to the UFC for one of the biggest matches of his career. Penn fought the reigning UFC welterweight champion Matt Hughes. After just four and a half minutes and another rear naked choke submission, Penn became the UFC welterweight champion.

In 2004 and 2005, Penn once again fought outside the UFC. He won three out of four MMA fights, including two against members of the Gracie family. In 2006, he returned to the UFC. In 2008, Penn defeated Joe Stevenson to become the UFC lightweight champion. He became just the second fighter in UFC history to win championships in two different weight classes.

Although Penn lost an attempt to win a second welterweight championship, he successfully defended his lightweight title three times. He then lost the belt as well as a rematch to Frank Edgar during two close matches.

Despite losing the belt, Penn remains an important figure in the world of MMA. He is hailed as one of the greatest submission fighters in UFC today. He's also the only fighter in UFC history to fight in four different weight classes.

CHAPTER 3

BRAZILIAN JIU-JITSU STEP-BY-STEP

"Power of mind is infinite while brawn is limited."—Koichi Tohei

MMA fights feature a mixture of martial arts that focus on both stand-up and ground styles. Some fighters have incredible striking abilities and can win many fights on their feet. More often than not, however, MMA fighters end up grappling and fights often go to the ground. At that point, there's no better martial art to know than Brazilian jiu-jitsu.

Every MMA fighter can benefit from at least a little Brazilian jiu-jitsu knowledge. At the very least, it can help a fighter to recognize dangerous moves before an opponent has a chance to complete them. But the more a fighter knows about the martial art, the more he or she can apply during a match.

Brazilian jiu-jitsu offers many opportunities to take advantage of an opponent's weaknesses. Takedowns quickly force opponents to the mat and into dangerous positions. Sweeps allow a fighter to quickly change a bad position to a dominant one. Chokes and joint locks, when properly applied, can bring a fight to an abrupt end. Even holds, which don't necessarily bring an end to a fight, can tire out opponents who struggle to get free.

CROSS SIDE/SIDE CONTROL

With your opponent on his back, kneel perpendicular to him and place your left hand snugly under his head.

Turn your face away from opponent to protect the face.

Brazilian jiu-jitsu offers something for every situation.

The photos in this chapter demonstrate the basic moves of Brazilian jiu-jitsu. The best way to practice these moves is with a partner. However, it's best to go slow to avoid injuries. It's always best to have the guidance of a trained martial artist. Some of the techniques shown here might be too hard for beginners. Never use these techniques to hurt others.

With left knee in position, slide right knee toward opponent's right hip.

Add pressure on opponent's face with your left shoulder.

Place your right hand on opponent's left hip.

KNEE TO BELLY

While having opponent in cross side/side control position, maneuver your right knee onto opponent's belly.

Position your left hand on opponent's left shoulder and your right hand on opponent's left hip.

SIT-UP SWEEP

Firmly grab back of opponent's left elbow with left hand.

Bend both knees and place feet flat on floor. Using your feet and upper back, raise pelvis and hips.

Using your body weight, apply pressure on opponent's torso.

Shift right hip and thrust, taking opponent with you.

With your opponent's palms positioned on your chest, bring your left hip forward while swinging your right arm back in a "windmill" fashion.

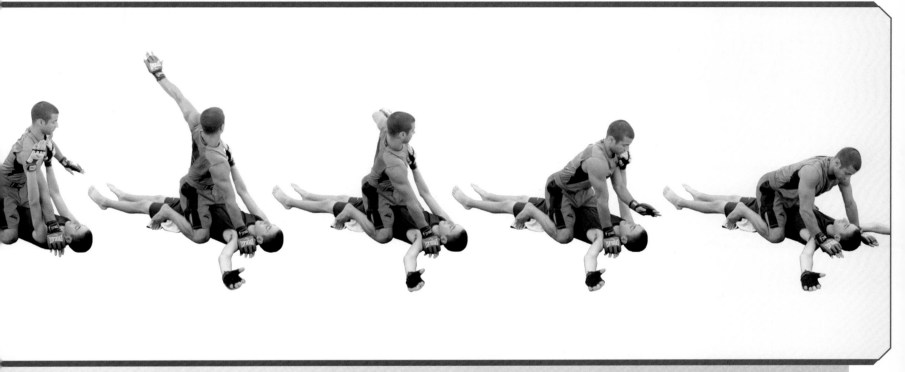

As your right arm completes a 360-degree "windmill" swing, slide your right hand between your opponent's arms, forcing his left hand off your chest.

Hold your opponent down by placing both hands firmly on his shoulders.

GUILLOTINE

Use left arm to wrap around neck by
scooping over and behind it.

ARM BAR

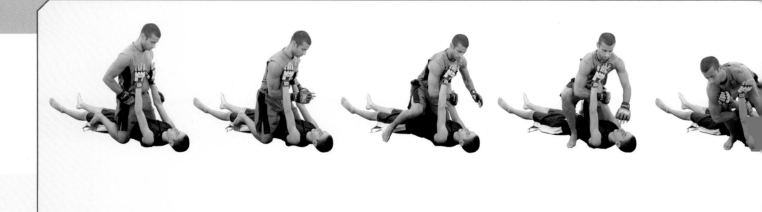

While opponent has both hands on your chest, wrap right arm
around opponent's right arm, gripping opponent's right elbow.

Bring your right knee up and position right foot flat on floor,
pressing right heel to opponent's left hip.

Squeeze opponent's neck with your left arm and grab your left wrist with right hand, locking the hold.

Wrap your legs around opponent's torso and lean back.

Use right foot as a lever to swing (lasso) left foot over opponent's head until both feet are firmly planted on floor to the left of your opponent.

Fall backward and pull opponent's right arm toward you until it's securely locked between your legs with opponent's thumb pointing to ceiling.

33

From mount position, shift shoulders down toward opponent.

Slide left arm underneath opponent's head and press your left shoulder firmly against opponent's right chin.

Grab your right bicep.

Reach your right hand across to your left shoulder and squeeze your elbows together while applying downward pressure.

Shift body up toward opponent and unlock your legs from opponent's torso.

Wrap right arm over opponent's right arm and grab your left wrist to lock the hold.

Turn right with opponent's locked arm and tighten your legs around opponent's torso.

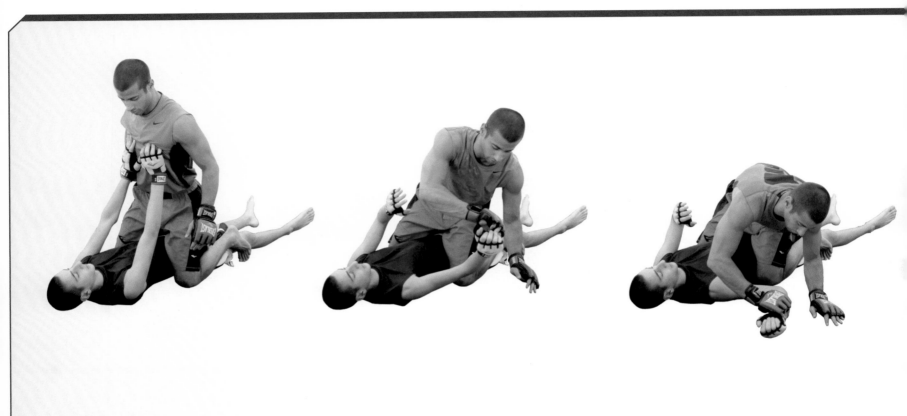

Place right hand on opponent's right wrist, pinning it to the floor.

Position your right elbow to opponent's ear to restrain movement while looking away from opponent to protect face.

Weave left hand between both your and your opponent's right arm and grab your wrist.

Sweep opponent's arm like a broom so that opponent's elbow is pointing to ceiling.

GLOSSARY

armbar A joint lock that affects the arm.

capoeira A combination martial art and dance form that originated in Brazil.

counterattack An attack made in response to an attack made by an opponent.

discipline A controlled and orderly state.

dojo A building where martial arts training takes place.

dominant In control over another.

grapple To struggle with an opponent in close, hand-to-hand combat.

guard A position where one fighter is lying on his or her back with an opponent between the legs.

joint lock A grappling move that involves forcing a joint to bend or twist farther than it can naturally move, causing pain.

judo A combat sport, similar to jiu-jitsu, that emphasizes quick movements and throws.

leverage The use of an opponent's own movements and body parts to control him or her.

mount A position on top of an opponent's stomach, side, or back.

practitioner Someone who participates in an activity or profession.

prestigious Having a high status.

prodigy Someone who shows exceptional talent at an early age.

prohibited Not allowed.

sambo A style of wrestling similar to judo and jiu-jitsu.

sensei A black-belt instructor.

submission A move that causes an opponent to admit defeat.

supplement To improve something by adding something to it.

sweep A move that allows a fighter to move from the guard to a dominant position.

unanimous Agreed upon by all.

veteran Someone who has a considerable amount of experience in something.

FOR MORE INFORMATION

Canadian National Martial Arts Association
1-3946 Quadra Street
Victoria, BC V8X 1J6
Canada
(250) 479-7686
Web site: http://www.cnmaa.com
The Canadian National Martial Arts Association is an organization that seeks to unify martial arts athletes and communities across Canada.

Gracie Barra
14988 Sand Canyon Avenue, Studio 1
Irvine, CA 92618
(949) 795-5257
Web site: http://www.graciebarraamerica.com
Gracie Barra is the U.S. headquarters of one of the largest and most traditional Brazilian jiu-jitsu schools in the world. Carlos Gracie Jr. is the founder and head instructor.

Gracie Jiu-Jitsu Academy

3515 Artesia Boulevard
Torrance, CA 90504
(877) 472-2430
Web site: http://www.gracieacademy.com
This is the U.S. headquarters for the famous Gracie
Academy.

International Brazilian Jiu-Jitsu Federation

Av Comandante Júlio de Moura 276
Barra da Tijuca
Rio de Janeiro, Brazil
Web site: http://www.ibjjf.org
The International Brazilian Jiu-Jitsu Federation is an
organization created by Carlos Gracie Jr. to represent
the sport of Brazilian jiu-jitsu around the world.

Judo Canada

212-1725 St. Laurent
Ottawa, ON K1G 3V4
Canada
(613)-738-1200
Web site: http://www.judocanada.org
Judo Canada is the national governing body for the sport
of judo in Canada.

U.S. Martial Arts Association

8011 Mariposa Avenue
Citrus Heights, CA 95610
(916) 727-1486
Web site: www.mararts.org
The U.S. Martial Arts Association is an organization that
aims to unify all American martial arts.

WEB SITES

Due to the changing nature of Internet links,
Rosen Publishing has developed an online list
of Web sites related to the subject of this book.
This site is updated regularly. Please use this link
to access the list:

http://www.rosenlinks.com/mma/jiu

FOR FURTHER READING

Barnes, Dawn. *Night on the Mountain of Fear.* New York, NY: Scholastic, 2006.

Ellis, Carol. *Judo and Jujitsu.* New York, NY: Marshall Cavendish Benchmark, 2011.

Ellis, Carol. *Wrestling.* New York, NY: Marshall Cavendish Benchmark, 2011.

Haney, Johannah. *Capoeira.* New York, NY: Marshall Cavendish Benchmark, 2012.

Ollhoff, Jim. *Grappling.* Edina, MN: ABDO Publishing, 2008.

Ollhoff, Jim. *Martial Arts Around the Globe.* Edina, MN: ABDO Publishing, 2008.

O'Shei, Tim. *Jujitsu.* Mankato, MN: Capstone Press, 2009.

Rielly, Robin L. *Karate for Kids.* Clarendon, VT: Tuttle Publishing, 2004.

Scandiffio, Laura. *The Martial Arts Book.* New York, NY: Annick Press, 2003.

Snowden, Jonathan, and Kendall Shields. *The MMA Encyclopedia.* Toronto, ON, Canada: ECW Press, 2010.

Webster-Doyle, Terrence. *Breaking the Chains of the Ancient Warrior: Tests of Wisdom for Young Martial Artists.* Middlebury, VT: Martial Arts for Peace Association, 1996.

Wells, Garrison. *Brazilian Jiujitsu: Ground-Fighting Combat.* Minneapolis, MN: Lerner Publications, 2011.

Wells, Garrison. *Mixed Martial Arts: Ultimate Fighting Combinations.* Minneapolis, MN: Lerner Publications, 2011.

Wells, Garrison. *Tae Kwon Do: Korean Foot and Fist Combat.* Minneapolis, MN: Lerner Publications, 2011.

Wiseman, Blaine. *Ultimate Fighting.* New York, NY: Weigl Publishers, 2011.

BIBLIOGRAPHY

BJJHeroes.com. "Roger Gracie." June 7, 2010. Retrieved September 14, 2011 (http://www.bjjheroes.com/bjj-fighters/roger-gracie-bio).

BJJHeroes.com. "Ronaldo Souza 'Jacare.'" February 10, 2010. Retrieved September 25, 2011 (http://www.bjjheroes.com/bjj-fighters/ronaldo-souza-jacare-fighter-wiki).

BJJHeroes.com. "Shinya Aoki." June 19, 2011. Retrieved September 25, 2011 (http://www.bjjheroes.com/bjj-fighters/shinya-aoki).

Carrasco, Pedro. "BJ Penn Bio." BJPenn.com. Retrieved September 8, 2011 (http://bjpenn.com/bio.php).

Dzida, Sarah, et al, eds. *The Ultimate Guide to Brazilian Jiu-Jitsu*. Valencia, CA: Black Belt Books, 2008.

Encarnacao, Jack. "The Unlikely Heir." Sherdog.com. Retrieved September 8, 2011 (http://www.sherdog.com/news/articles/1/The-Unlikely-Heir-29686).

Gracie Jiu-Jitsu Academy. "The Origin of Jiu-Jitsu." Retrieved September 9, 2011 (http://www.gracieacademy.com/generations_helio.asp).

International Brazilian Jiu-Jitsu Federation. "The History of Brazilian Jiu-Jitsu." Retrieved September 9, 2011 (http://www.ibjjf.org/jjh.htm).

International Brazilian Jiu-Jitsu Federation. "Regulations and Rules of Jiu-Jitsu." Retrieved September 14, 2011 (http://www.ibjjf.org/rules.htm).

RogerGracie.com. "About Roger Gracie." Retrieved September 14, 2011 (http://www.rogergracie.com/about_roger_gracie).

Rousseau, Robert. "A History and Style Guide of MMA." About.com. Retrieved September 13, 2011 (http://martialarts.about.com/od/styles/a/mma.htm).

Sherdog.com. "Roger Gracie." Retrieved September 14, 2011 (http://www.sherdog.com/fighter/Roger-Gracie-19854).

Sherdog.com. "Ronaldo 'Jacare' Souza." Retrieved September 25, 2011 (http://www.sherdog.com/fighter/Ronaldo-Souza-8394).

Sherdog.com. "Shinya 'Tobikan Judan' Aoki." Retrieved September 25, 2011 (http://www.sherdog.com/fighter/Shinya-Aoki-10774).

Simco, Gene. *Brazilian Jiu-Jitsu Basics*. New York, NY: Citadel Press Books, 2004.

Simco, Gene. "Jiu-Jitsu History." Jiu-jitsu.net. Retrieved September 9, 2011 (http://www.jiu-jitsu.net/history.shtml).

Strickland, Jonathan. "How the Ultimate Fighting Championship Works." HowStuffWorks.com, May 1, 2007. Retrieved September 8, 2011 (http://entertainment.howstuffworks.com/ufc4.htm).

Walder, Marc. *Essential Brazilian Jiu-Jitsu*. Champaign, IL: Human Kinetics, 2008.

Walter, Donald F., Jr. "Mixed Martial Arts: Ultimate Sport, or Ultimately Illegal?" GrappleArts.com, December 12, 2003. Retrieved September 22, 2011 (http://www.grapplearts.com/Mixed-Martial-Arts-1.htm).

INDEX

ABOUT THE AUTHOR

Greg Roza has been writing and editing educational materials for twelve years. He has a master's degree from SUNY Fredonia and lives in Hamburg, New York, with his wife and three kids. He recently earned his purple belt in Isshinryu karate and is a white belt in Brazilian jiu-jitsu. Roza and his children are all on the road to becoming karate black belts.

ABOUT BEN DANIEL

Ben Daniel was born in Israel and raised in Margate, New Jersey. He has a bachelor of science degree in biology from Richard Stockton College of New Jersey. He has been training under Master Mal Perkins in American tae kwon do since age six and has also practiced Brazilian jiu-jitsu and hapkido each for nine years. Since receiving his first-degree black belt at sixteen, he has been teaching martial arts to students of all ages. He is now a third-degree black belt and is in training for his fourth-degree master's belt. He resides in New York, where he works as a professional personal trainer.

PHOTO CREDITS